Where Poppies Grow

Quilts and Projects Honoring Those Who Served in World War I

BY DENNIELE BOHANNON AND JANICE BRITZ

KANSAS CITY STAR
QUILTS
Continuing the Tradition

Where Poppies Grow
Quilts and Projects Honoring Those
Who Served in World War I
By Denniele Bohannon and Janice Britz

Editor: Edie McGinnis
Designer: Heather Shaw
Photography: Aaron T. Leimkuehler
Illustration: Eric Sears
Technical Editor: Jane Miller
Photo Editor: Jo Ann Groves

Published by:
Kansas City Star Books
1729 Grand Blvd.
Kansas City, Missouri, USA 64108

Kansas City Star Quilts moves quickly to publicize
corrections to our books. You can find corrections at www.
KansasCityStarQuilts.com, then click on "Corrections."

First edition, first printing
ISBN: 978-1-61169-140-5

Library of Congress Control Number: 2014945902

Printed in the United States of America by Walsworth
Publishing Co., Marceline, Missouri

To order bulk copies, call (816) 234-4473; for single copies,
call (816) 234-4242.

KANSAS CITY STAR
QUILTS
Continuing the Tradition

ACKNOWLEDGEMENTS

Thank you to Doug Weaver, Edie
McGinnis, Jo Ann Groves, Eric
Sears, Aaron Leimkuehler, Jane
Miller and Heather Shaw, the team
at The Kansas City Star.

Thank you, Deb Rowden for your
encouragement. Ruth Blades,
Robert Blades, Mary Blades Toney,
George Blades, Helen Blades Tilton,
Richard Townsend O'Kell, Victoria
O'Kell Liston and Allison Crowe,
all descendants of Pearl Townsend
O'Kell Blades, thank you for sharing
your memories, photos and the
cemetery tours.

A special thanks to Moda fabrics at
Modafabrics.com for supplying the
fabric for our quilt, Remembering
Almo.

About the Authors

DENNIELE BOHANNON

Denniele has been teaching quilting in the adult education program for the Harrisonville School District since 2007. She is a member of AQS, NQA and MOKA. Denniele and her husband, Meryl, reside in Harrisonville, Missouri. They have five grown children and three grandchildren.

From Denniele Bohannon:
Thank you to Kandi Dillon, the pattern tester for Remembering Almo, Dianne Barnden, for piecing A Mother's Remembrance and Janice Britz for working on this project. Ginger Friesz, Veronica Johnson, Donna Crow and Shari Gilliam, the sewing girls who help me. To my husband, kids and grandkids, thank you for being you and loving me – fabric, threads and all!

JANICE BRITZ

Janice made her first two quilts in 1976, and then took a break for a few years. After raising her family and working as a Shelter Insurance agent, she resumed quilting in 2007. She is now retired and enjoying her family. Her other passion is beekeeping and operating Bee Merry Farms, selling honey and beeswax. Janice and her husband, Tom, have three children and six grandchildren. Janice is one of four authors who contributed to "Stories in Stitches" published by Kansas City Star Quilts.

From Janice Britz:
Denniele, it was a privilege to read Almo's letters and work with you to complete this book. To my family, thank you for your love and patience – love you more!

Introduction

The year 2014 marks the 100th anniversary of the beginning of World War I. With the assassination of Archduke Franz Ferdinand in Sarajevo on June 28, 1914, as a catalyst, "The Great War" was set in motion. Never before had so many nations been prepared to embark upon battles that would encompass so much territory and end with the loss of so many lives.

European leaders chose up sides quickly after the assassination. The Allies — Russia, Great Britain and France – faced the central powers of Germany, Austria-Hungary and Turkey. The war spread beyond Europe as the warring factions called upon their colonies and other allies for help. In 1917, America joined the fray.

One of the doughboys who was sent "over there" was Almo Ebenezer O'Kell, a congenial, well-liked young man who hailed from Quincy, Illinois. He served as a medic with Field Hospital No. 3 of the First Division under the command of General John J. Pershing.

O'Kell had an ex-wife and an 8-year-old son, Townsend, living in Hamilton, Missouri. He often wrote to Townsend, as well as his family and friends. His letters and photos have been preserved by his family and are a remarkable first-hand account of his life as a soldier.

His great-granddaughter, Denniele O'Kell Bohannon of Louanna Mary Quilt Design, Harrisonville, Missouri, and Janice Britz of Bee Merry Farms, Peculiar, Missouri, were inspired by O'Kell's WWI experiences and designed the 2014 Kansas City Star Block-of-the-Month quilt, Remembering Almo, in honor of the 100th anniversary of The Great War.

Contents

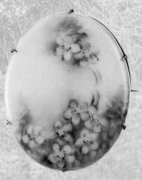

Remembering Almo, designed by Denniele Bohannon and Janice Britz, pieced by Denniele Bohannon and quilted by Angela Walters of Quilting is My Therapy.

Remembering Almo

Quilt Size: 72" x 83"

Fabric Requirements
- ⅔ yard assorted reds
- ⅔ yard assorted blues
- ½ yard brown*
- 7" x 9" gold
- ¾ yard green
- 3 ½ yards of background

Borders
- 2 ¼ yards red
- 2 ½ yards of background
- 10 ½" x 22" blue
- 20" fusible web

Other Supplies
- 1 yard fusible web
- black embroidery thread (optional)

*From the brown fabric, using your favorite method, make 372" of ¼" finished bias tape. Cut into 31" increments. Set aside.

WWI Tribute Quilt, designed by Denniele Bohannon and Janice Britz,
pieced by Janice Britz and quilted by Angela Walters of Quilting is My Therapy.

WWI Tribute Quilt

Quilt Size: 64" x 82"

The WWI Tribute quilt uses the same 12 block patterns as Remembering Almo. The blocks are set together differently, and this quilt gives you another option for borders. You will find the finishing instructions on pages 56 – 59.

Fabric Requirements

- 1 yard background fabric for pieced blocks
- ⅔ yard of assorted red fabrics for pieced blocks
- ⅔ yard of assorted blue fabrics for pieced blocks

Alternate Blocks, Borders, Sashing and Binding

- 4 ⅓ yards of background fabric
- 1 ¾ yards of red fabric
- 1 ½ yards of blue fabric

Photo: "Zwischen Vesle und Aisne" by Unknown. Wikimedia Commons

Block 1 - Father's Choice

Photo: "WWI 42nd Division burial party" by (Unknown) Wikimedia Commons

Almo married Pearl Townsend in 1907, and their son, Townsend, was born in 1909, in Quincy, Illinois. Pearl and Townsend often went to Hamilton, Missouri, to visit her mother, so Almo started writing to his son shortly after his birth.

"Dear Son, This is your first card, with love from your papa."

Almo was not often pleased with her absence, as one of his letters attests: "Now Pearl I think you had better hurry up and come home as I can't stand it any longer. I tell you it is fierce to keep away that long. Kiss the dear baby for me."

Before he sailed for France, Almo was at Ft. Oglethorpe, Georgia, the war induction and processing center. In November 1917, he wrote to 8-year-old Townsend: "Papa wants you to be a good boy and mind your mama. She will tell you all about me some day. Now baby, Papa thinks of you all the time and when this war is over, over there, [I] will come and see you."

Almo understood that many men would sacrifice their lives, "But it is very doubtful if I will come back to this country again, only one way. But Baby, remember your father lost his life in the fight for freedom for you because it would mean [America would] come under the rule of Germany. Of course it can't last long but [there] will be lots of us that won't come back. But if I do, I want to come and see you."

Almo gave a final exhortation to Townsend before he sailed: "So you be a good boy and Papa will be happy for you. Now Townsend go to school every day and study hard while papa is over in Germany fighting. I am sending you the last picture I had taken so you can keep it and remember daddy as long as you live."

Townsend O'Kell, at age eight.

7

BLOCK 1 - FATHER'S CHOICE
BLOCK SIZE: 14" FINISHED

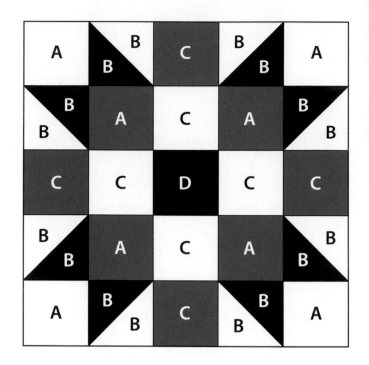

CUTTING DIRECTIONS

From the red fabric, cut:
- 4 – 3" squares (B)
- 1 – 2 ½" square (D)

From the blue fabric, cut:
- 4 – 2 ¼" squares (A)
- 4 – 2 ½" x 2 ¼" rectangles (C)
- 1 – 2 ½" square - Apply fusible to the square, and cut one circle using template two.

From the background fabric, cut:
- 4 – 2 ¼" squares (A)
- 4 – 3" squares (B)
- 4 – 2 ½" x 2 ¼" rectangles (C)
- 2 – 3 ½" x 9 ½" rectangles
- 2 – 3 ½" x 15 ½" rectangles

From the green fabric, apply fusible and cut:
- 34 leaves using template three

From the gold fabric, apply fusible and cut:
- 1 star using template one

31" of previously made brown bias tape

CONSTRUCTION

Sew a blue A square to either side of a background C rectangle as shown. Make two rows like this.

Make another row by sewing a background C rectangle to either side of a red D square. Make one row.

Sew the three rows together to make a 9-patch block.

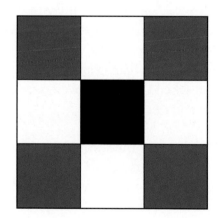

Draw a diagonal line from corner to corner on the reverse side of 4 background B squares. Place a background B square atop a red B square with right sides facing; stitch ¼" on both sides of the drawn line. Cut apart on the line. Press toward the red. Trim down to a 2 ¼" square. Make eight half-square-triangle units.

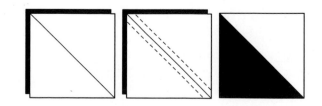

Sew a half-square triangle unit to either side of a blue C rectangle. Make four.

Stitch a row to either side of the center 9-patch as shown.

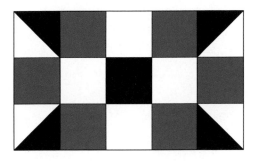

Add a background A square to either end of the two remaining rows, and stitch one to the top and one to the bottom of the block.

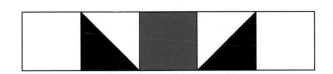

Sew a 3 ½" x 9 ½" background rectangle to the top and bottom of the center block.

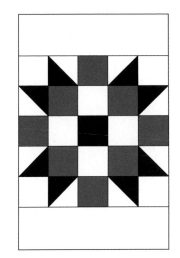

Add a 3 ½" x 15 ½" background rectangle to the left and right sides. The block will be trimmed to 14 ½" after the appliqué is complete.

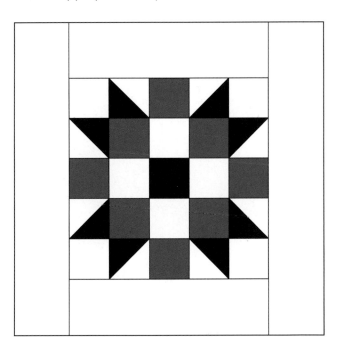

Refer to the placement guide on page 77, and mark the position of the bias stem. Stitch the stem in place. Center the blue circle on the stem, fuse and stitch in place. Place the gold star on the blue circle so the two arms lay just above the stem and the top arm is centered on the circle. Fuse and stitch in place. Refer to the placement guide, and position the leaves on the stem so they are pleasing to your eye; fuse and stitch in place. Backstitch U.S. on the gold star, if desired. Trim the block to 14 ½." You will find the templates on page 77.

9

Block 2 – Love Entangled

Almo joined the Army in 1916, long before the Selective Service Act of 1917, when many men were drafted into the war. He trained at the Jefferson Barracks Military Post located on the Mississippi River south of St. Louis. He was a raw recruit when tensions between the United States and Mexico were at a breaking point. He joined Field Hospital No. 3 at Columbus, New Mexico, and entered Mexico with the punitive expedition commanded by General John Pershing.

Back home, Almo's wife, Pearl, was struggling to raise her son, Townsend, by herself. Pearl's adoptive mother, Lorinda Townsend, was not pleased with her daughter's husband, Almo. He was a light-hearted charmer who enjoyed life … nothing but a dandy in Lorinda's eyes.

Pearl's petition for divorce, filed after Almo joined the Army, stated "defendant is a stout able-bodied man and very efficient as a druggist clerk and in other capacities and is able and does earn a good wage when disposed to work, but being of a roving, unsettled disposition, remains but short time in any one place."

While it is uncertain who first filed for the divorce that was eventually granted, Lorinda's meddling was clearly evident. In spite of the circumstances, Almo continued to write to Pearl and Townsend. Much to his disappointment, she never replied. Not once.

Almo's wife, Pearl, is shown in her Hamilton High School graduation picture. The two married shortly after she graduated.

BLOCK 2 - LOVE ENTANGLED
BLOCK SIZE: 14" FINISHED

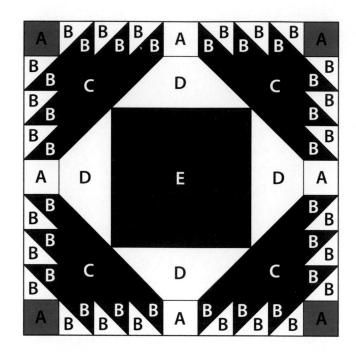

CUTTING DIRECTIONS

From the red fabric, cut:

- 12 – 2 ¼" squares (B)
- 1 – 4 ½" square (E)

From the light blue fabric, cut:

- 4 – 1 ½" squares (A)

From the dark blue fabric, cut:

- 2 – 3 ⅞" squares (C) - Cut each square once diagonally.
- 1 – 2" square - Apply fusible web and cut one circle using template two.

From the background fabric, cut:

- 4 – 1 ½" squares (A)
- 12 – 2 ¼" squares (B)
- 4 pieces using template (D)
- 2 – 3 ½" x 9 ½" rectangles
- 2 – 3 ½" x 15 ½" rectangles

From the green fabric, apply fusible web and cut:

- 34 leaves using template three

From the gold fabric, apply fusible web and cut:

- 1 star using template one

31" of previously made brown bias tape

CONSTRUCTION

Sew a background D piece to the left and right of the red E square. Press toward the D pieces.

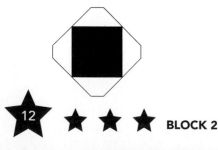

Sew a background D piece to the top and bottom of the E square. Press toward the D pieces.

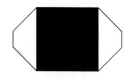

Sew a blue C triangle to opposite sides as shown. Press toward the blue triangles.

Add a C blue triangle to the remaining sides. Press toward the blue triangles.

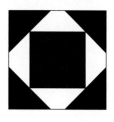

Draw a diagonal line from corner to corner on the reverse side of 12 background B squares. Place a background B square atop a red B square with right sides facing. Stitch ¼" on both sides of the drawn line. Cut apart on the line. Press toward the red. Make 24 half-square triangles, and trim each to 1 ½".

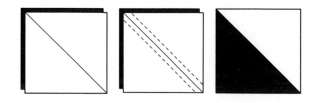

12   ★ ★ ★   **BLOCK 2**

Sew three half-square triangles together as shown. Make four. Press the seams open.

Stitch a background A square on the right as shown. Make four. Press the seams open.

Sew three half-square triangles together as shown. Make four. Note that the half-square triangles are oriented differently from the first set. Press the seams open.

Stitch the half-square triangles to the right side of the background square. Press the seams open. Make four.

Stitch a row to the left and right side of the pieced center as shown. Note that the base of the red triangles is sewn next to the pieced center. Press toward the center.

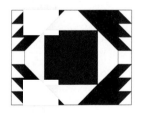

Sew a blue A square to each end of the row. Make two. Press toward the blue.

Add the remaining rows to the top and bottom. Press toward the center.

Sew a 3 ½" x 9 ½" background rectangle to the top and bottom of the center block. Press toward the background rectangles.

Sew a 3 ½" x 15 ½" background rectangle to the sides of the center block. Press toward the background rectangles.

Refer to the placement guide on page 77, and mark the position of the bias stem. Stitch the stem in place. Center the blue circle on the stem, fuse and stitch in place. Place the gold star on the blue circle so the two arms lay just above the stem and the top arm is centered on the circle. Fuse and stitch in place. Refer to the placement guide, and position the leaves on the stem so they are pleasing to your eye; fuse and stitch in place. Backstitch U.S. on the gold star, if desired. Trim the block to 14 ½". You will find the appliqué templates and the piecing template on page 77.

Block 3 - Dog Tooth Violet

O'Kell shared his experiences about the punitive expedition in Mexico to capture Francisco "Pancho" Villa with his son, Townsend, by sending him picture postcards of the outposts. One postcard showed a tall, slender tree stripped of its branches that was used as a pole to fly the American flag. O'Kell wrote, "This flag was raised at Nocozari on Sept. 20, 1916, by the U.S. Army - Papa."

Another postcard pictured a shaggy dog in front of an encampment. "This dog followed us from Columbus, New Mexico, on April 12, 1916, into Mexico, and came out with us on February 5, 1917. He is with us now - Papa."

O'Kell wrote to folks back home, and often his letters would be quoted in The Quincy Daily Journal. On July 6, 1916, the headline read, "Former Quincyan with Expedition Now Gives 'Inside' Belief." According to the story, "The American punitive expedition in Mexico will be withdrawn by August 1, according to the belief of Almo (Bunny) O'Kell, formerly employed here at the Christie Drug Store, and now with the hospital division of the expedition 'somewhere in Mexico.'" Unfortunately, O'Kell was wrong, and the expedition was recalled to Fort Bliss. On February 7, 1917, General Pershing marched into El Paso, officially ending the failed campaign.

The dog that followed Field Hospital No. 3 during the Mexican Punitive Expedition.

BLOCK 3 - DOG TOOTH VIOLET
BLOCK SIZE: 14" FINISHED

CUTTING DIRECTIONS

From the red fabric, cut:

- 4 – 2 ⅝" squares (B)
- 4 – triangles using template (D)

From the blue fabric, cut:

- 4 – 3 ⅜" x 1 ¾" rectangles (E and Er) - With right sides facing, cut from corner to corner once on the diagonal.
- 1 – 2" square - Apply fusible web and cut one circle using template two.

From the background fabric, cut:

- 1 – 2 ⅝" square (B)
- 4 – triangles using template (A)
- 4 – triangles using template (Ar)
- 4 – triangles using template (C)
- 2 – 3 ½" x 9 ½" rectangles
- 2 – 3 ½" x 15 ½" rectangles

From the green fabric, apply fusible web and cut:

- 34 leaves using template three

From the gold fabric, apply fusible web and cut:

- 1 star using template one

31" of previously made brown bias tape

CONSTRUCTION

Stitch a blue E triangle to the left of the C background triangle and a blue Er triangle to the right. Press toward the blue. Make four.

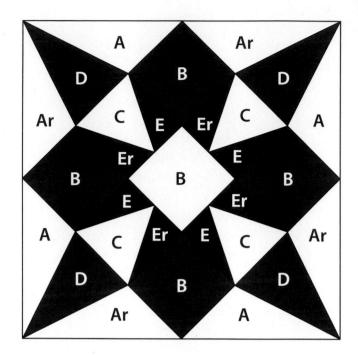

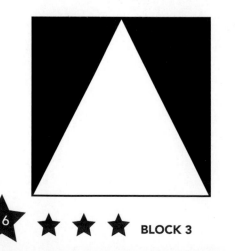

Sew a red B square to either side of an E/C/Er unit. Make two sets. Then sew an E/C/Er unit to either side of the background B square. Press toward the E/C/Er units. Create a 9-patch block as shown.

Sew an A background triangle to the right side of the D triangle and an Ar on the left, creating a corner unit. Press toward the background. Make four.

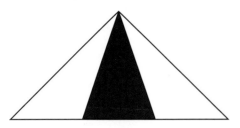

Stitch a corner unit to the opposite sides of the center square. Then add the remaining corner units. Press toward the corner.

Sew a 3 ½" x 9 ½" background rectangle to the top and bottom of the center block. Press toward the background. Then sew a 3 ½" x 15 ½" background rectangle to the sides of the center block. Press toward the background.

Refer to the placement guide on page 77, and mark the position of the bias stem. Stitch the stem in place. Center the blue circle on the stem, fuse and stitch in place. Place the gold star on the blue circle so the two arms lay just above the stem and the top arm is centered on the circle. Fuse and stitch in place. Refer to the placement guide, and position the leaves on the stem so they are pleasing to your eye; fuse and stitch in place. Backstitch U.S. on the gold star, if desired. Trim the block to 14 ½". You will find the appliqué templates on page 77 and the piecing templates on page 78.

Block 4 – Ladies Delight

Almo had been back in El Paso, Texas, only a few months when the United States declared war on Germany. General Pershing, commander of The American Expeditionary Forces, organized the First Division, a formation of experienced, regular soldiers in preparation for mobilizing the Army. Almo was going "over there" once the Army had raised, trained and equipped a larger force.

Meanwhile, Almo met Tillie Trummer. After a short courtship, they were married on September 22, 1917. The El Paso Herald reported, "At the home of Rev. P.R. Knickerbocker, on Sunday evening, Miss Tillie Trummer and Almo E. O'Kell of the field hospital corps were quietly married, the bride wearing a blue tailleur. Until ordered elsewhere, the newlyweds will be at home at 1115 North Ochoa Street."

Almo wrote home to his mother, Susie, about his marriage to Tillie: "I will send Tillie's picture to Quincy. It was taken of her when she was 19 years old and she was much heavier then. So you take good care of it for me and, Mother, get me a copy of my divorce and send to Tillie for me. Do this at once."

Almo later realized he had made a mistake in marrying Tillie before he left for war. In August of 1918, he wrote to Pearl's mother, Lorinda, "Tell Pearl I am glad she is doing so nicely and hope she will always. And that she won't make a mistake as I did before I left the states. But things will happen that way now and then. Also tell Pearl that if she hasn't anything else to do why she might write a few lines."

Almo was one of the experienced regular soldiers of the First Division of the American Expeditionary Forces.

BLOCK 4 – LADIES DELIGHT
BLOCK SIZE: 14" FINISHED

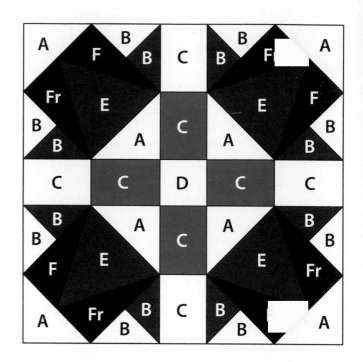

CUTTING DIRECTIONS

From the red fabric, cut:

- 2 – 3 ⅛" squares (B) - Cut the squares from corner to corner twice on the diagonal.
- 4 triangles using template E

From the dark blue fabric, cut:

- 4 – 4" x 2" rectangles (F) and (Fr) - With right sides together, cut from corner to corner once on the diagonal.

From the light blue fabric, cut:

- 4 – 2 ⅜" x 2" rectangles (C)
- 1 – 2" square - Apply fusible web, and cut one circle using template two.

From the background fabric, cut:

- 4 – 2 ¾" squares (A) - Cut from corner to corner once on the diagonal.
- 2 – 3 ⅛" squares (B) - Cut the squares from corner to corner twice on the diagonal.
- 4 – 2 ⅜" x 2" rectangles (C)
- 1 – 2" square (D)
- 2 – 3 ½" x 9 ½" rectangles
- 2 – 3 ½" x 15 ½" rectangles

From the green fabric, apply fusible web and cut:

- 34 leaves using template three

From the gold fabric, apply fusible web and cut:

- 1 star using template one

31" of previously made brown bias tape

CONSTRUCTION

Stitch a background C rectangle to a light blue C rectangle. Press toward the light blue. Make four. Stitch a unit to either side of a background D square. Press toward the light blue. You will have two C/C units left. Put them aside for the moment.

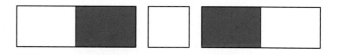

Sew an F dark blue triangle to one side of a red E triangle and an Fr to the other side. Press toward the dark blue. Make four.

Sew a B red triangle to a B background triangle. Press toward the red. Make eight. **Note:** four of the red triangles will be on the right, the remaining ones on the left.

Stitch the B/B triangles to the F/E/Fr unit as shown. Press toward the B triangles. Add an A background triangle to the two remaining corners. Press toward the background corners. Make four.

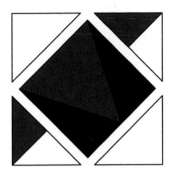

Assemble the rows as shown below. Press to the center rectangles. Then stitch the rows together to complete the center of the block.

Sew a 3 ½" x 9 ½" background rectangle to the top and bottom of the center block. Press toward the background. Add a 3 ½" x 15 ½" background rectangle to each side. Press toward the background.

Refer to the placement guide on page 77, and mark the position of the bias stem. Stitch the stem in place. Center the blue circle on the stem, fuse and stitch in place. Place the gold star on the blue circle so the two arms lay just above the stem and the top arm is centered on the circle. Fuse and stitch in place. Refer to the placement guide, and position the leaves on the stem so they are pleasing to your eye; fuse and stitch in place. Backstitch U.S. on the gold star, if desired. Trim the block to 14 ½". You will find the appliqué templates on page 77 and the piecing templates on page 78.

Block 5 – The Airplanes

The USS Mallory, troop transport ship.
Photo: National World War I Museum, Kansas City, Missouri USA

Units of the First Division began shipping out June 1917 and throughout the remainder of the year. Almo traveled from El Paso to Ft. Oglethorpe, Georgia, and embarked at Hoboken, New Jersey, arriving in France on December 22, 1917. Almo wrote, "We had two storms at sea. The big boat rolled and tossed for almost two days at a time."

The Division assembled at Gondrecourt, France, where Field Hospital No. 3 operated the camp hospital until April 1918. Almo and his unit then began moving with the front line functioning as a triage. They were placed at Cheppy, and while there, they were so severely shelled, they had to move the wounded.

About Cheppy, Almo wrote, "After taking the hospital, which was an old German dugout for the serious wounded, we put up tents. The first three days and nights not a man of the company went to sleep as we were too busy.

"On the morning of the 4th of October [1918], we were shelled for about one hour. The first shell hit a touring car but didn't explode. The second hit within 50 feet of the main entrance of the dugout. The third one exploded directly on top of the dugout and caved it in for about 8 feet. Then in the afternoon about 40 airplanes came over but didn't do any bombing. The Germans that was doing the firing on us was found to be 2 kilometers in our own lines. The Germans didn't know that the rest had retreated so were soon made prisoners."

BLOCK 5 – THE AIRPLANES
BLOCK SIZE: 14" FINISHED

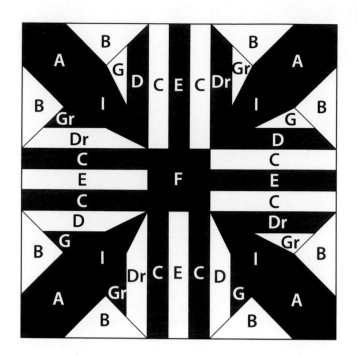

CUTTING DIRECTIONS

From the red fabric, cut:

- 4 – 4 ⅛" x 1 ⅛" (C)
- 2 pieces using template (D)
- 2 pieces using template (Dr)
- 2 – 4 ⅛" x 1" rectangles (E)
- 2 triangles using template (G)
- 2 triangles using template (Gr)

From the blue fabric, cut:

- 4 pieces using template (A)
- 1 – 2 ¼" square (F)
- 4 triangles using template (I)
- 1 – 2" square - Apply fusible web, and cut one circle from template two.

From the background fabric, cut:

- 2 – 3 ⅝" squares (B) - Cut the squares from corner to corner twice on the diagonal.
- 4 – 4 ⅛" x 1 ⅛" (C)
- 2 pieces using template (D)
- 2 pieces using template (Dr)
- 2 – 4 ⅛" x 1" rectangle (E)
- 2 triangles using template (G)
- 2 triangles using template (Gr)
- 2 – 3 ½" x 9 ½" rectangles
- 2 – 3 ½" x 15 ½" rectangles

From the green fabric, apply fusible web and cut:

- 34 leaves using template three

From the gold fabric, apply fusible web and cut:

- 1 star using template one

31" of previously made brown bias tape

Note: All four corners are made using the same pieces but have different color placement. Refer to the labeled diagram for color placement.

CONSTRUCTION

Sew a G triangle to the shorter side of a D piece. Press toward the darker fabric. Sew a Gr triangle to the shorter side of a Dr piece. Press toward the dark. Sew a G/D unit to a blue I triangle, then add the Gr/Dr unit.

Sew a background B triangle to both sides of a blue A piece. Press toward the blue. Sew the B/A/B unit to the G/D/I/Dr/Gr unit as shown below. Make four corner units. Again, refer to the labeled diagram above for color placement.

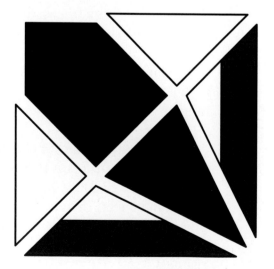

Sew a red C rectangle to both sides of a background E rectangle. Press toward the red. Make two. Sew a background C rectangle to either side of a red E rectangle. Press toward the red. Make two.

Sew a corner unit to either side of a striped unit to make the top row of the block. Make two. Sew a striped unit to either side of the center blue F square. Sew the three rows together as shown.

Sew a 3 ½" x 9 ½" background rectangle to the top and bottom of the center block. Press toward the background fabric. Sew a 3 ½" x 15 ½" background rectangle to the sides of the center block. Press toward the background.

Refer to the placement guide on page 77, and mark the position of the bias stem. Stitch the stem in place. Center the blue circle on the stem, fuse and stitch in place. Place the gold star on the blue circle so the two arms lay just above the stem and the top arm is centered on the circle. Fuse and stitch in place. Refer to the placement guide, and position the leaves on the stem so they are pleasing to your eye; fuse and stitch in place. Backstitch U.S. on the gold star, if desired. Trim the block to 14 ½". You will find the appliqué templates on page 77 and the piecing templates on page 79.

Block 6 - My Country

In early November, German delegates crossed over the Allied lines seeking a truce. The Armistice that allowed peace negotiations to take place was signed Tuesday, November 11, 1918, at 11 a.m.

The combat mission of the American Expeditionary Forces was over. It became their duty to move into Central Germany to disarm and disband the German forces. Pershing had to build the German occupying force using the troops who were under his command. On November 14, 1918, the Third U.S. Army was designated as the Army of Occupation with Major General Joseph T. Dickman as commander.

On Sunday, November 17, 1918, the American and Allied forces began to slowly move toward Germany. Soldiers marched in worn-out boots and uniforms through mud and rain. They had come straight from combat and were in dire need of having their equipment refurbished. The few trucks they had at their disposal often broke down, and they were stuck for hours waiting for repair.

Almo's unit, Field Hospital 3, was moved by truck. They arrived at their temporary camp, a bombed-out French barracks, late one night. He wrote home and said, "We saw the campfires the troops had built in the camp and for the last 10 months they couldn't even have a light at night in their sleeping quarters unless they were about 100 miles from the front line." None of them had been that far away.

Compiegne, France, Nov. 11, 1918. Allied soldiers outside a railroad car in which the Armistice was signed. Pictured in the center are General Maxime Weygand of France, Admiral Wemyss of Great Britain and Marshal Foch of France.
National World War I Museum, Kansas City, Missouri USA

BLOCK 6 - MY COUNTRY
BLOCK SIZE: 14" FINISHED

CUTTING DIRECTIONS

From the red fabric, cut:
- 2 – 2 ½" squares (C) - Cut the squares from corner to corner twice on the diagonal.
- 1 – 1 ⅞" square (F)

From the blue fabric, cut:
- 4 pieces using template B
- 4 pieces using template D
- 1 – 2" square - Apply fusible web, and cut one circle from template two.

From the background fabric, cut:
- 2 – 3 ¾" squares (A) - Cut the squares from corner to corner once on the diagonal.
- 1 – 2 ½" squares (C) - Cut the square from corner to corner twice on the diagonal.
- 2 – 3 ⅜" squares (E) - Cut the squares from corner to corner once on the diagonal.
- 2 – 3 ½" x 9 ½" rectangles
- 2 – 3 ½" x 15 ½" rectangles

From the green fabric, apply fusible web and cut:
- 34 leaves using template three

From the gold fabric, apply fusible web and cut:
- 1 star using template one

31" of previously made brown bias tape

CONSTRUCTION

Stitch a background A triangle to the longer side of a blue B piece. Add a background E triangle. Press toward the blue piece. Make four of these corner units.

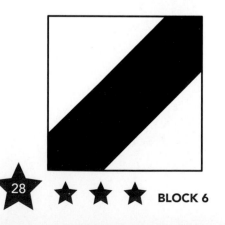

Sew a red C piece to a blue D piece. Stitch a background C piece to a red C piece, and stitch in place as shown. Press all seam allowances toward the darker fabric. Make four.

Sew a corner unit to either side of a D/C/C/C unit. Press toward the blue. Make two.

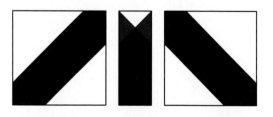

Stitch a D/C/C/C unit to either side of the red F square. Press toward the red square.

Sew the three rows together as shown.

Sew a 3 ½" x 9 ½" background rectangle to the top and bottom of the center block. Press toward the background. Sew a 3 ½" x 15 ½" background rectangle to the sides of the center block. Press toward the background.

Refer to the placement guide on page 77, and mark the position of the bias stem. Stitch the stem in place. Center the blue circle on the stem, fuse and stitch in place. Place the gold star on the blue circle so the two arms lay just above the stem and the top arm is centered on the circle. Fuse and stitch in place. Refer to the placement guide, and position the leaves on the stem so they are pleasing to your eye; fuse and stitch in place. Backstitch U.S. on the gold star, if desired. Trim the block to 14 ½". You will find the appliqué templates on page 77 and the piecing templates on page 79.

FORT OGLETHORPE
GEORGIA.

Block 7 - French Star

The Nov. 22 Stars and Stripes headline read, "Letters Home Now May Mention Town and Give All News," and Almo soon started telling the folks back home his whereabouts. He had survived some of the heaviest fighting of the war, and in one letter he wrote, "We sure did run a foot race with the Kaiser."

The First Division led the American Army of Occupation as it began moving into Germany. Many of the soldiers stayed in private homes in towns they passed through. Almo commented on his accommodations in a letter, saying, "… so you see we live in good homes in Germany" and that they had "the best of rooms."

On Dec. 4, Field Hospital No. 3 entered the town of Traben-Trarbach in Germany. Almo stayed at the home of a wealthy wine merchant while waiting for his orders. While there, he wrote, "I sure had some time! He had two daughters and two sons and we were visiting nearly every night to some other dealer's home."

Postcard of Traben-Trarbach, Germany, where Almo lodged with a wine merchant.

BLOCK 7 - FRENCH STAR
BLOCK SIZE: 14" FINISHED

CUTTING DIRECTIONS

From the red fabric, cut:

- 1 – 4 ¼" square (E)
- 1 – 2 ¾" square (B) - Cut the square from corner to corner twice on the diagonal.

From the blue fabric, cut:

- 4 pieces using template (A)
- 4 pieces using template (Ar)
- 1 – 2" square - Apply fusible web, and cut one circle from template two.

From the background fabric, cut:

- 4 – 3 ⅛" squares (F)
- 1 – 5" square (C) - Cut the square from corner to corner twice on the diagonal.
- 1 – 3" x 8" rectangle - Apply fusible web, and cut eight ovals using template D.
- 2 – 3 ½" x 9 ½" rectangles
- 2 – 3 ½" x 15 ½" rectangles

From the green fabric, apply fusible web and cut:

- 34 leaves using template three

From the gold fabric, apply fusible web and cut:

- 1 star using template one

31" of previously made brown bias tape

CONSTRUCTION

Sew a blue A piece to red B triangle. Press toward the blue. Sew a blue Ar to the right side of a background C triangle. Press toward the blue. Stitch the two together as shown to make an A/Ar/B/C unit. Make four.

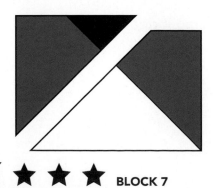

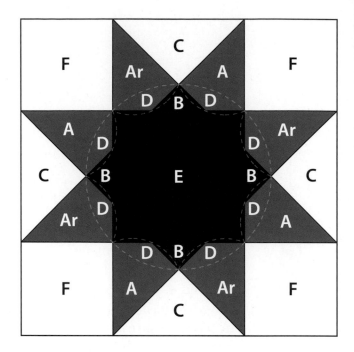

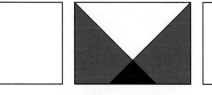

Stitch an F background square to either side of an A/Ar/B/C unit. Press toward the background squares. Make two rows.

Stitch an A/Ar/B/C unit to either side of a red E square. Press toward the red square.

Sew the three rows together.

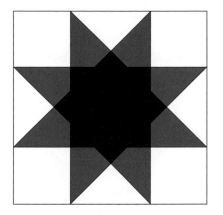

Place the ends of the D ovals at the intersections of the blue triangles. The fuller side of the D oval is toward the center. Fuse and appliqué the ovals in place as shown.

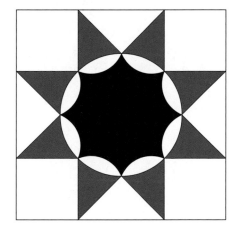

Sew a 3 ½" x 9 ½" background rectangle to the top and bottom of the center block. Press toward the background. Sew a 3 ½" x 15 ½" background rectangle to the sides of the center block. Press toward the background.

Refer to the placement guide on page 77, and mark the position of the bias stem. Stitch the stem in place. Center the blue circle on the stem, fuse and stitch in place. Place the gold star on the blue circle so the two arms lay just above the stem and the top arm is centered on the circle. Fuse and stitch in place. Refer to the placement guide, and position the leaves on the stem so they are pleasing to your eye; fuse and stitch in place. Backstitch U.S. on the gold star, if desired. Trim the block to 14 ½". You will find the appliqué templates on page 77 and the piecing templates on page 80.

Block 8 – Winged Square

Bridge over the Rhine River.

Orders came to Field Hospital 3 on Dec. 11 to proceed to the Rhine River. The trucks first had to cross the Moselle River before they could reach the Rhine. The shortest route involved crossing over a pontoon bridge at Traben-Trarbach. The trucks were too heavy and had to be rerouted to the town of Cochem to cross the Moselle. "It sure was beautiful to see but awfully cold!"

Almo arrived in Koblenz on Dec. 12, 1918. "We had to await orders to cross and stayed there about an hour. We crossed the Rhine as the First Sanitary Train of the First Division at 11:53 am. We had only seven minutes in which to cross as the First Division had to be across by noon.

"We have the honor of being the first U.S. troops that ever crossed the Rhine. It is not known in history of any other that ever crossed it before in the history of the German empire."

BLOCK 8 - WINGED SQUARE
BLOCK SIZE: 14" FINISHED

CUTTING DIRECTIONS

From the red fabric, cut:

- 4 – 2 ⅛" squares (C)
- 36 – 1" squares (F)
- 4 – 1 ⅛" x 3 ⅝" rectangles (G)

From the blue fabric, cut:

- 1 – 3 ⅝" square (E)
- 36 – 1" squares (F)
- 1 – 2" square - Apply fusible web, and cut one circle using template two.

From the background fabric, cut:

- 2 – 3 ⅛" squares (A) - Cut the squares from corner to corner once on the diagonal.
- 2 – 3 ½" squares (B) - Cut the squares from corner to corner twice on the diagonal.
- 8 – 1" x 3 ⅝" rectangles (D)
- 2 – 3 ½" x 9 ½" rectangles
- 2 – 3 ½" x 15 ½" rectangles

From the green fabric, apply fusible web and cut:

- 34 leaves using template three

From the gold fabric, apply fusible web and cut:

- 1 star using template one

31" of previously made brown bias tape

CONSTRUCTION

Sew a background D rectangle to both sides of a red G rectangle. Press toward the red. Make four. Set two DGD units aside, and sew a red C square to both ends of the remaining DGD units.

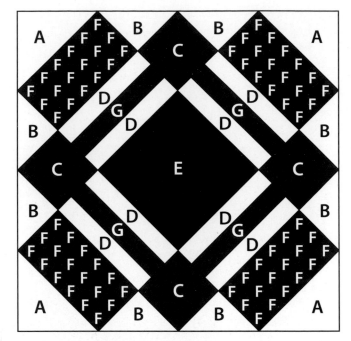

Add a background B triangle to the two DGD/C units as shown. Press toward the triangle.

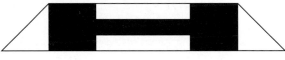

Sew a red F square to a blue F square. Make nine pairs. Stitch three pairs together to make a row containing six squares. Sew the three rows together, creating a checkerboard. Press all seams open. Make four.

Making sure a blue square is in the lower left corner, sew a background A triangle to the long side of the checkerboard unit. Press toward the triangle. Make four. Set two aside and add a background B triangle to both ends of the checkerboard. Press toward the B triangle.

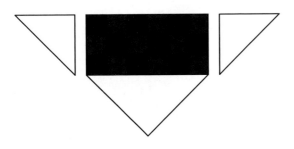

Stitch together the remaining DGD units, checkerboard/A units and blue E square to make the center row. Lay out and stitch the rows together as shown.

Sew a 3 ½" x 9 ½" background rectangle to the top and bottom of the center block. Press toward the background. Sew a 3 ½" x 15 ½" background rectangle to the sides of the center block. Press toward the background.

Refer to the placement guide on page 77, and mark the position of the bias stem. Stitch the stem in place. Center the blue circle on the stem, fuse and stitch in place. Place the gold star on the blue circle so the two arms lay just above the stem and the top arm is centered on the circle. Fuse and stitch in place. Refer to the placement guide, and position the leaves on the stem so they are pleasing to your eye; fuse and stitch in place. Backstitch U.S. on the gold star, if desired. Trim the block to 14 ½". You will find the appliqué templates on page 77.

Block 9 – Red Cross

After arriving in Koblenz, Almo traveled about 30 miles northeast to Höhr, Germany, on Dec. 13, 1918. While there, he sent a postcard home to his son, Townsend, and his ex-wife, Pearl. "I sure have seen some fine scenery and nice people. We travel by trucks so of course see more than most of the boys."

He stayed one day in Höhr-Grenzhausen (formerly known as Höhr in 1918) and then traveled to Dernbach, where they set up a hospital in a Catholic Sisters Hospital for the Poor. "We are using part of it and have a very nice place. I am in charge of all the wards and wardmasters and all the clothing of the patients. The sisters say they can't see why we work so hard keeping the floors clean. You see, it has been awful weather since we came up here a week ago now. It is either raining or snowing or both most of the time."

Almo was keenly aware that Christmas was approaching, and he would spend it in Germany, away from Townsend again. Almo wrote, "But I only hope I will be [home] so I can send you something for the next one if I am lucky enough to come out of this war and back to the states." This was the third year that he missed Christmas with Townsend.

Almo did manage to send a postcard to Townsend on Christmas Eve. "Dear Baby, Just a Christmas card as this is all we can get here. -- With love and kisses, Papa."

Red Cross parades were held in towns and cities across the United States during World War I. Almo's son, Townsend, holds the flag at the front of his school's parade.

BLOCK 9 - RED CROSS
BLOCK SIZE: 14" FINISHED

CUTTING DIRECTIONS

From the red fabric, cut:

- 4 – 2 ¼" squares (A)
- 4 – 2 ½" x 2 ¼" rectangles (D)
- 1 – 2 ½" square (E)

From the blue fabric, cut:

- 4 pieces using template (C)
- 1 – 2" square - Apply fusible web, and cut one circle using template two.

From the background fabric, cut:

- 6 – 2 ⅝" squares (B) - Cut the squares from corner to corner once on the diagonal.
- 4 – 2 ½" x 2 ¼" rectangles (D)
- 2 – 3 ½" x 9 ½" rectangles
- 2 – 3 ½" x 15 ½" rectangles

From the green fabric, apply fusible web and cut:

- 34 leaves using template three

From the gold fabric, apply fusible web and cut:

- 1 star using template one

31" section of previously made brown bias tape

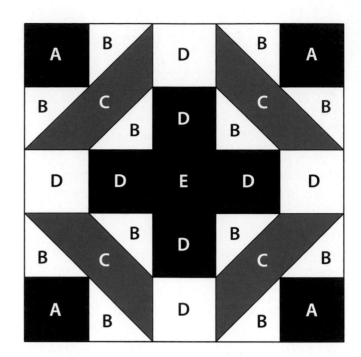

CONSTRUCTION

Stitch a red D rectangle to a background D rectangle. Press toward the red. Make four. Set two aside. Stitch a DD unit to either side of the red E square. Press away from the center square. This is the center row. Set aside for the moment.

Sew a background B triangle to two sides of a red A square. Press toward the triangles. Add a blue C piece and another background B triangle as shown. Make four of these corner units.

Sew a corner unit to either side of a DD unit. Press toward the center. Make two rows like this.

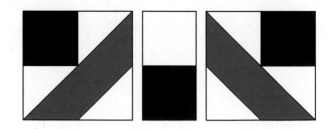

Sew the three rows together to complete the center of the block.

Sew a 3 ½" x 9 ½" background rectangle to the top and bottom of the center block. Add a 3 ½" x 9 ½" background rectangle to the left and right sides. The block will be trimmed to 14 ½" after the appliqué is complete.

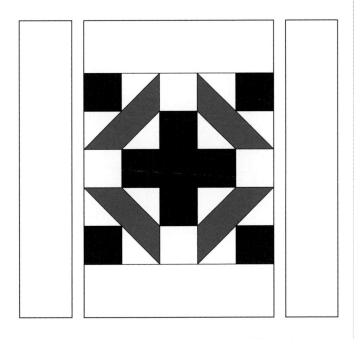

Refer to the placement guide on page 77, and mark the position of the bias stem. Stitch the stem in place. Center the blue circle on the stem, fuse and stitch in place. Place the gold star on the blue circle so the two arms lay just above the stem and the top arm is centered on the circle. Fuse and stitch in place. Refer to the placement guide, and position the leaves on the stem so they are pleasing to your eye; fuse and stitch in place. Backstitch U.S. on the gold star, if desired. Trim the block to 14 ½". You will find the appliqué templates on page 77 and the piecing templates on page 80.

★ ★ ★ ★ 41

Block 10 - Dove in the Window

Almo wrote a few letters home after the New Year and said that he was doing well. His health quickly deteriorated when he fell ill with appendicitis. Even though his appendix was removed, Almo died of peritonitis on January 12, 1919, in Koblenz.

Almo's letters had often expressed his premonitions about never returning home and seeing his son, Townsend, again. Phrases such as, "If I ever return home again …" and "it is doubtful I will come home but if I do …" were a constant refrain. His final journey ended in Quincy, Illinois, just a little more than a year after he had shipped out from Hoboken, New Jersey.

Only one of Almo's death notices listed him from El Paso, Texas, with Tillie as his survivor. Missouri and Illinois death notices listed his survivors as "his wife and son who make their home in Hamilton, Missouri."

A letter written by Almo arrived posthumously to the Congregational Sunday School in Quincy thanking them for some gifts he had received. He was represented on the honor roll of the Sunday school, and the blue star before his name was changed to gold.

Flowers from Field Hospital No. 3 were among the graveside arrangements for Sergeant First Class Almo E. O'Kell.

BLOCK 10 - DOVE IN THE WINDOW
BLOCK SIZE: 14" FINISHED

CUTTING DIRECTIONS

From the red fabric, cut:

- 8 triangles using template (C)

From the blue fabric, cut:

- 2 – 3 ¼" squares (A)
- 1 diamond using template (E)
- 2 pieces using template (F)
- 1 – 2" square - Apply fusible web, and cut one circle using template two.

From the background fabric, cut:

- 2 – 3 ¼" squares (A)
- 8 triangles using template (B)
- 2 triangles using template (D)
- 2 triangles using template (Dr)
- 2 – 3 ½" x 9 ½" rectangles
- 2 – 3 ½" X 15 ½" rectangles

From the green fabric, apply fusible web and cut:

- 34 leaves using template three

From the gold fabric, apply fusible web and cut:

- 1 star using template one

31" section of previously made brown bias tape

CONSTRUCTION

Stitch a Dr triangle to opposite sides of the E diamond. Press toward the diamond.
Stitch a D triangle to an F piece. Press toward piece F. Make two and stitch them to the top and bottom of the Dr/E unit as shown.

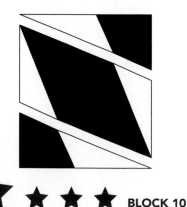

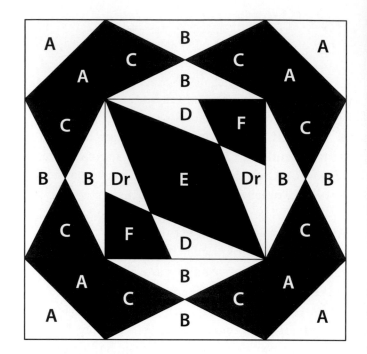

Stitch a background B triangle to a red C triangle. Make eight and join two together as shown to create a rectangle. Make four.

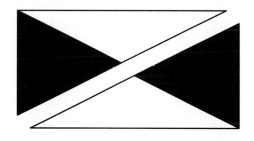

Draw a diagonal line of the back of each background A square. Layer it with a blue A square with right sides together. Stitch ¼" on both sides of the line. Cut on the drawn line. Open and press toward the blue. Trim each square to measure 2 ¾". You will have four half-square triangles.

Stitch a half-square triangle to both ends of the BC rectangle. Make two rows like this.

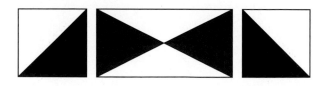

Stitch a BC rectangle to either side of the center square.

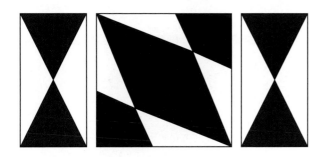

Sew the three rows together to complete the center of the block.

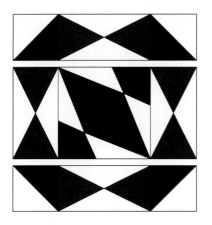

Sew a 3 ½" x 9 ½" background rectangle to the top and bottom of the center block. Press toward the background. Sew a 3 ½" x 15 ½" background rectangle to the sides, and press toward the background.

Refer to the placement guide on page 77, and mark the position of the bias stem. Stitch the stem in place. Center the blue circle on the stem, fuse and stitch in place. Place the gold star on the blue circle so the two arms lay just above the stem and the top arm is centered on the circle. Fuse and stitch in place. Refer to the placement guide, and position the leaves on the stem so they are pleasing to your eye; fuse and stitch in place. Backstitch U.S. on the gold star, if desired. Trim the block to 14 ½". You will find the appliqué templates on page 77 and the piecing templates on page 81.

Due to his parents' divorce, Almo divided his time between Hamilton, Missouri, and Quincy, Illinois. He was a congenial man who seemed to be at home wherever his feet were planted. The Army took him from Missouri to Texas, Mexico, Georgia, France and, finally, Germany.

Almo's mother, Susie, wasn't the type to interfere in her grown son's life. She tended to stay in the shadows until she was needed. In one of his letters, he wrote, "Say mama, when we get over across why [don't] you have the boys send me some smoking as it cost the moon across there."

He was devoted to his mother and wanted to provide for her before he sailed for Europe. "Well mama, I took out $5000 worth of insurance for you today." Once the Armistice was signed and military censorship was relaxed, Almo's letters home became more detailed.

Mrs. O'Kell received the telegram that Almo's body had reached Hoboken. His remains arrived in Quincy, Illinois, at 9:30 p.m. on Saturday, Jan. 18, 1919. His funeral was held the next day in the family home, and he was buried in Greenmount Cemetery in Quincy, Illinois.

Sadly, Mrs. O'Kell had joined the legions of gold star mothers across the nation.

Almo's mother, Susie O'Kell with her grandson, Townsend.

BLOCK 11 – MOTHER'S DREAM
BLOCK SIZE: 14" FINISHED

CUTTING DIRECTIONS

From the red fabric, cut:
- 4 – 3 ½" x 1 ½" rectangles (C)
- 4 – 2 ⅝" squares (D)

From the blue fabric, cut:
- 12 – 2" squares (B)
- 1 – 2 ⅝" square (D)
- 1 – 2" square - Apply fusible web, and cut one circle from template two.

From the background fabric, cut:
- 10 – 2 ⅜" squares (A) - Cut the squares from corner to corner once on the diagonal.
- 12 – 2" squares (B)
- 2 – 3 ½" x 9 ½" rectangles
- 2 – 3 ½" x 15 ½" rectangles

From the green fabric, apply fusible web and cut:
- 34 leaves using template three

From the gold fabric, apply fusible web and cut:
- 1 star using template one

31" section of previously made brown bias tape

CONSTRUCTION

You will need to make 24 blue/background half-square triangle units for this block. To make the half-square triangles, draw a diagonal line on the back of the background B squares. Sew ¼" on both sides of the diagonal line. Cut on the drawn line. Open and press toward the blue fabric and trim to 1½".

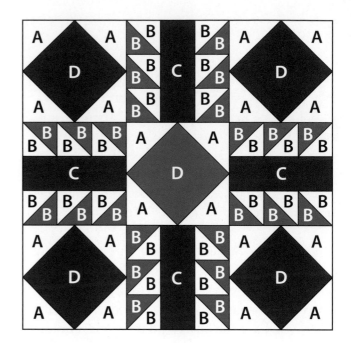

Sew three half-square triangles together as shown. Press the seams open. Make eight rows and sew a row to either side of a red C rectangle. Press toward the red. Make four.

Sew background A triangles to opposite sides of a red D square. Press toward the background. Repeat on the other two sides. Make four units using a red D square in the center and one unit using a blue center D square.

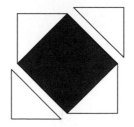

Sew the units into rows as shown. Sew the rows together to complete the center of the block.

Sew a 3 ½" x 9 ½" background rectangle to the top and bottom of the center block. Press toward the background. Sew a 3 1/2" x 15 1/2" background rectangle to the sides of the center block. Press toward the background.

Refer to the placement guide on page 77, and mark the position of the bias stem. Stitch the stem in place. Center the blue circle on the stem, fuse and stitch in place. Place the gold star on the blue circle so the two arms lay just above the stem and the top arm is centered on the circle. Fuse and stitch in place. Refer to the placement guide, and position the leaves on the stem so they are pleasing to your eye; fuse and stitch in place. Backstitch U.S. on the gold star, if desired. Trim the block to 14 ½". You will find the appliqué templates on page 77.

Block 12 – Heavenly Puzzle

One of the finest WWI monuments is the Liberty Memorial in Kansas City, Missouri. It houses the National WWI Museum. Before entering the museum proper, a person must cross over the glass-floored Paul Sunderland Bridge. Under the bridge is a field of poppies, 9,000 in all, each representing 1,000 lives lost in the Great War. In Memory Hall, the names of the 441 Kansas City-area residents who died while serving their country can be found on the four "We Are The Dead" bronze tablets. Sergeant First Class Almo E. O'Kell is listed as a noncommissioned officer.

In 1921, General Pershing, Lt. Gen. Baron Jacques of Belgium, Gen. Armando Diaz of Italy, Marshal Ferdinand Foch of France and Adm. Lord David Beatty of Great Britain were invited to attend the dedication ceremony of the construction site. It was the first time the five Allied Commanders had been together. They stood on a makeshift stage among other dignitaries in front of a crowd of nearly 100,000 people.

Construction began on the monument July 5, 1923. Delays and rising costs plagued the project. Even though the Memorial was still not complete, an extravagant dedication ceremony was planned and took place on Armistice Day 1926. At exactly 11 o'clock, a bell tolled denoting the hour the Armistice had been signed. President Coolidge began his speech dedicating the monument on the eighth anniversary of the end of the war.

Almo E. O'Kell's name is listed on one of the bronze tablets in Memory Hall at Liberty Memorial.

BLOCK 12 - HEAVENLY PUZZLE
BLOCK SIZE: 14" FINISHED

CUTTING DIRECTIONS

From the red fabric, cut:

- 4 pieces using template (A)
- 2 – 2 ⅝" squares (C) - Cut from corner to corner once on the diagonal.

From the blue fabric, cut:

- 4 pieces using template (B)
- 4 pieces using template (Br)
- 4 – 4 ⅛" x 2 ¼" rectangles (D)
- 1 – 2" square - Apply fusible web, and cut one circle using template two.

From the background fabric, cut:

- 4 – 2 ⅝" squares (C) - Cut from corner to corner once on the diagonal.
- 4 triangles using template (E)
- 1 – 2 ¼" square (F)
- 2 – 3 ½" x 9 ½" rectangles
- 2 – 3 ½" x 15 ½" rectangles

From the green fabric, apply fusible web and cut:

- 34 leaves using template three

From the gold fabric, apply fusible web and cut:

- 1 star using template one

31" section of previously made brown bias tape

CONSTRUCTION
Sew a red A piece to a blue B piece. Add a background C triangle. Press toward the blue. Sew a background E triangle to a blue Br piece, and add a background C triangle. Press toward the blue. Sew the two parts together as shown, and finish the corner unit by adding a red C triangle. Make four corner units.

Make the top and bottom row of the block by sewing a corner to either side of a blue D rectangle to create a row. Press toward the blue. Make the center row by stitching a blue D rectangle to either side of the F background square. Press toward the blue. Sew the three rows together as shown to complete the center of the block.

Sew a 3 ½" x 9 ½" background rectangle to the top and bottom of the center block. Press toward the background. Sew a 3 ½" x 15 ½" background rectangle to the sides of the center block. Press toward the background.

Refer to the placement guide on page 77, and mark the position of the bias stem. Stitch the stem in place. Center the blue circle on the stem, fuse and stitch in place. Place the gold star on the blue circle so the two arms lay just above the stem and the top arm is centered on the circle. Fuse and stitch in place. Refer to the placement guide, and position the leaves on the stem so they are pleasing to your eye; fuse and stitch in place. Backstitch U.S. on the gold star, if desired. Trim the block to 14 ½". You will find the appliqué templates on page 77 and the piecing templates on page 82.

Almo O'Kell in his dress uniform.

53

FINISHING INSTRUCTIONS
FOR REMEMBERING ALMO

CUTTING DIRECTIONS

From the background fabric, cut:

- 1 – 14 ½" strip across the width of fabric – Sub-cut into the following pieces:
    - 8 – 14 ½" x 2 ½" rectangles (A)
    - 4 – 5 ⅜" squares (G)

Cut the remaining pieces on the lengthwise grain of fabric.

- 2 – 74 ½" x 3 ½" strips (F)
- 2 – 62 ½" x 4 ½" strips (C)
- 2 – 54 ½" x 3 ½" strips (D)
- 1 – 54 ½" x 9 ½" strip (E)
- 3 – 46 ½" x 2 ½" strips (B)

Trace 14 border stars onto fusible web, press onto background fabric and cut.

From the red border fabric, cut on the lengthwise grain of fabric.

- 4 – 74 ½" x 3 ½" strips (F)
- 2 – 54 ½" x 3 ½" strips (D)

Using the template provided, trace 3 swags onto fusible web, press onto the red fabric and cut.

From the blue fabric, cut:

- 2 – 10" squares (H)

Refer to the diagram and make four horizontal rows of three blocks, adding the A pieces as shown. Stitch a background B strip to the bottom of each of the first three rows. Stitch the rows together. Add a background C strip to either side of the center, and add a background E piece to the bottom.

Appliqué the three red swags to the top edge of a background D strip and stitch to the quilt top.

Stitch a red F strip to either side of a background F strip. Draw a diagonal line on a background G square. Place on one corner of the sewn strips with right sides facing. Stitch on the line and trim. Repeat on the other corner. Make two and sew to either side of the quilt.

Appliqué seven border stars to each of the blue H squares. Trim to 9 ½". Stitch a red D strip to either side of a background D strip. Sew a blue H square to each end of the strip set and stitch to the top of the quilt. You will find the templates on page 82.

Border Star Template

Border Star Template

FINISHING INSTRUCTIONS FOR WWI TRIBUTE QUILT

CUTTING DIRECTIONS
Note: WOF indicates width of fabric.

ALTERNATE SETTING BLOCKS: 9" FINISHED
From the red fabric, cut:

- 12 – 2" squares (C)

From the background fabric, cut:

- 12 – 2" squares (C)
- 12 – 3 ½" squares (B)
- 12 – 3 ½" x 9 ½" rectangles (A)

SASHING
From the background fabric, cut:

- 96 – 1 ¾" x 9 ½" rectangles (A)

From the blue fabric, cut:

- 48 – 1" x 9 ½" rectangles (B)

CORNERSTONES AND PIECED BORDERS
From the red fabric, cut:

- 105 – 1 ½" squares (D)

From the blue fabric, cut:

- 210 – 1" x 2 ½" rectangles (B)
- 210 – 1" x 1 ½" rectangles (C)

From the background fabric, cut:

- 210 – 1" x 2 ½" rectangles (B)
- 210 – 1" x 3 ½" rectangles (A)

SIDE SETTING CORNERSTONES
From the red fabric, cut:

- 7 – 1 ⅞" squares (E)

From the blue fabric, cut:

- 14 – 1"x 2 ⅞" rectangles (F)
- 14 – 1" x 1 ⅞" rectangles (G)

From the background fabric, cut:

- 14 – 1" x 2 ⅞" rectangles (F)
- 14 – 1" x 3 ⅞" rectangles (H)

SIDE SETTING AND CORNER TRIANGLES
From the background, cut:

- 3 – 14" squares – Cut the squares from corner to corner twice on the diagonal for the side triangles. You will have two triangles left over.
- 2 – 7 ¼" squares – Cut the squares from corner to corner once on the diagonal for the corner triangles.

BORDERS AND BINDING
From the blue fabric, cut:

- 7 – 1 ½" x WOF for inner borders

From the red fabric, cut:

- 4 – 1" x WOF for side borders
- 3 – 1 ½" x WOF for top and bottom borders
- 8 – 2" x WOF for outer borders
- 8 – 2 ½" x WOF strips for straight binding

CONSTRUCTION

Sew all pieced blocks, omitting the 3 ½" x 9 ½" background rectangles and appliqué pieces.

ALTERNATE SETTING BLOCKS
Sew a red C square to a background C square. Press toward the red. Make two. Sew two C/C units together to make the center 4-patch. Sew a B background square to either end of the 4-patch then sew an A background rectangle to either side as shown below. Make six.

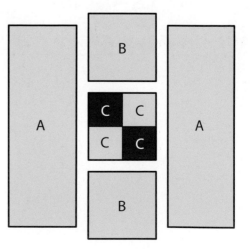

SASHING STRIPS

Sew a background A rectangle to either side of a blue B rectangle. Press toward the background. Make 48.

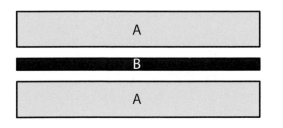

CORNERSTONES AND PIECED BORDER

Sew a blue C rectangle to the top and bottom of a red D square. Press toward the blue. Sew a blue B rectangle to either side of the DC unit. Press toward the blue B. Sew a background B rectangle to the top and bottom of the DCB unit. Press toward the background.
Sew a background A rectangle to either side of the DCBB unit. Press toward the background. Make 105. Set aside 88 units for the pieced border.

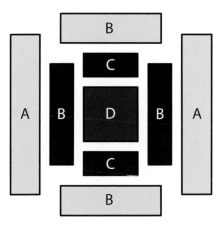

SIDE SETTING CORNERSTONES

Sew a blue G rectangle to the top and bottom of a red E square. Press toward the blue. Sew a blue F rectangle to either side of the EG unit. Press toward the blue. Sew a background F rectangle to the top and bottom of the EFG unit. Press toward the background. Sew a background H rectangle to either side of the EFFG unit. Press toward the background. Make seven. Cut from corner to corner once on the diagonal.

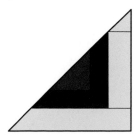

Refer to the diagram and sew the sashing units to the blocks making rows as shown. Sew a side or end triangle to each end of the row. Note the orientation of the alternate setting blocks. Press all in one direction.

Refer to the diagram and sew the cornerstones and sashing units together. Sew a diagonally-cut cornerstone on the end of each row. Note the orientation of the diagonally-cut cornerstone. Press in the opposite direction as you did the sashing.

New Year's greeting card found among O'Kell's letters.

BORDERS

Measure the quilt top through the center from top to bottom. Join the lengths of the 1 1/2" blue border strips to match the measurement. Sew to the sides of the quilt, pressing toward the border.

Measure the quilt top again through the center from side to side. Join the lengths of the 1 1/2" blue border strips to match the measurement. Sew one to the top and one to the bottom of the quilt. Press toward the border.

Repeat the process used for the first red border. Use the 1" strips for the side borders and the 1 1/2" strips for the top and bottom borders.

Sew together 24 of the pieced DCBB units along the seamless sides to make a side pieced border strip. Make 2. Sew one to either side of the quilt and press toward the red border.

Sew together 20 of the pieced DCBB units along the seamless sides to make the top and bottom pieced border strips. Make 2. Sew one to the top and one to the bottom of the quilt. Press toward the red border.

Measure the quilt top through the center from top to bottom. Join the lengths of the 2" red border strips to match the measurement. Sew to the sides of the quilt, pressing toward the red border.
Measure the quilt top again through the center from side to side. Join the lengths of the 2" red border strips to match the measurement. Sew one to the top and one to the bottom of the quilt. Press toward the border.

Layer with backing and batting, quilt and bind.

★ ★ ★ ★ 59

Designed and Pieced by Denniele Bohannon
Quilted by Angela Walters

Long Road Home

Quilt Size: 70" x 88"

Fabric Requirements

- 1 ¾ yards gold fabric
- 1 ¾ yards white fabric
- 5 ¾ yards blue fabric (includes binding)

CUTTING DIRECTIONS

From the gold fabric, cut:

- 136 – 3" squares (E)
- 17 – 5 ½" squares (F)
- 4 – 3 ½" squares (G)
- 42 – 2 ⅝" squares (L)

From the white fabric, cut:

- 304 – 1 ½" x 2" rectangles (B)
- 25 – 4 ¼" squares – Cut each square from corner to corner twice on the diagonal (N).
- 8 – 2 ½" strips WOF (outer border)

From the blue fabric, cut:

- 304 – 1" x 2" rectangles (A)
- 48 – 3 ½" squares (C)
- 48 – 5 ½" x 9 ½" rectangles (D)
- 4 – 6 ½" x 9 ½" rectangles (O)
- 6 – 6 ½" squares (H)
- 4 – 8 ¾" squares – Cut each square from corner to corner twice on the diagonal (J).
- 2 – 7 ¼" squares – Cut each square from corner to corner once on the diagonal (I).
- 3 – 9 ¾" squares – Cut each square from corner to corner twice on the diagonal (K).
- 12 – 7 ¼" squares – Cut each square from corner to corner twice on the diagonal (M).
- 10 pieces using template P
- 9 – 2 ½" strips WOF. Set aside to use for the binding.

Almo's letters were filled with fond memories of his homes in Quincy and Hamilton and his family. He never complained about the circumstance of war and had tender, comforting words for his family.

CONSTRUCTION

Stitch the long sides of a white B rectangle and a blue A rectangle together. Sew four AB units together to make a cross block. Make 76.

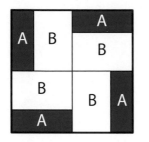

Using five cross blocks and four blue C squares, assemble a 9-patch as shown. Make eight.

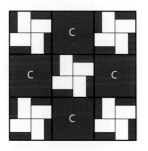

Stitch a cross block to both sides of a blue C square. Stitch to a blue O rectangle. Make four.

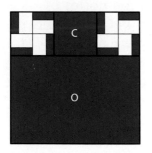

Stitch a cross block to a blue C square. Sew the cross/C unit to a blue H square. Stitch a cross block to both sides of a blue C square, and sew to the cross/C/H unit as shown below. Make six.

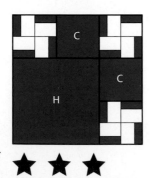

Stitch a cross block to the blue piece P. Add the blue K triangle as shown. Make 10.

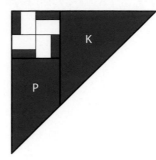

Draw a diagonal line from corner to corner on the back of the gold E squares. Place a gold E square on the corner of a blue D rectangle. Stitch on the drawn line. Trim to a ¼" seam, flip open and press. Place a gold E square on the opposite corner of the blue D rectangle. Stitch on the line, trim the seam, flip open and press. Make 44. Set 20 of these aside to use later. With the remaining 24, add gold E squares to the opposite end.

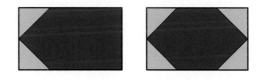

Sew a blue J triangle to opposite ends of a blue D rectangle. Stitch an I triangle to the side forming a corner. Make four.

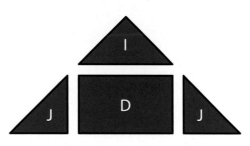

★ ★ ★

Using the diagram as guide, assemble the rows as shown. Stitch the assembled units and J/D/I triangles into rows as shown. Sew the rows together to form the center of the top.

Stitch a white N triangle to two sides of a gold L square as shown. Make 42. Stitch two white N triangles together as shown. Make eight.

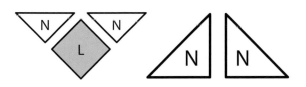

Sew 13 blue M triangles and 12 N/L/N units together to make a side border strip. Add an N/N unit to both ends of the strip. Make two. Stitch to either side of the quilt.

Sew 10 blue M triangles and nine N/L/N units together to make a top and bottom border strip. Add a N/N unit to both ends of the strip. Stitch a gold G square to both ends. Make two. Sew one to the top of the quilt and the other to the bottom.

Measure the length of the quilt. Sew enough white 2 1/2" strips together to equal that measurement. Make two, and sew one to the left and the other to the right side of the quilt. Measure the width of the quilt. Sew enough white 2 1/2" wide white strips together to equal that measurement. Sew one to the top and one to the bottom of the quilt. You can find the templates on page 83.

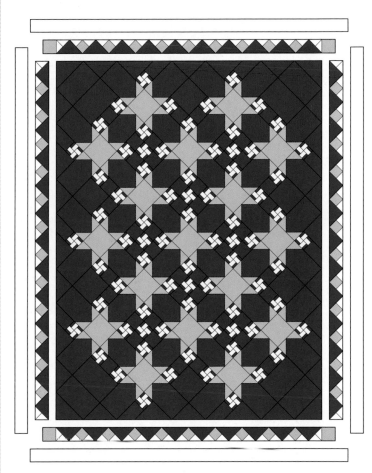

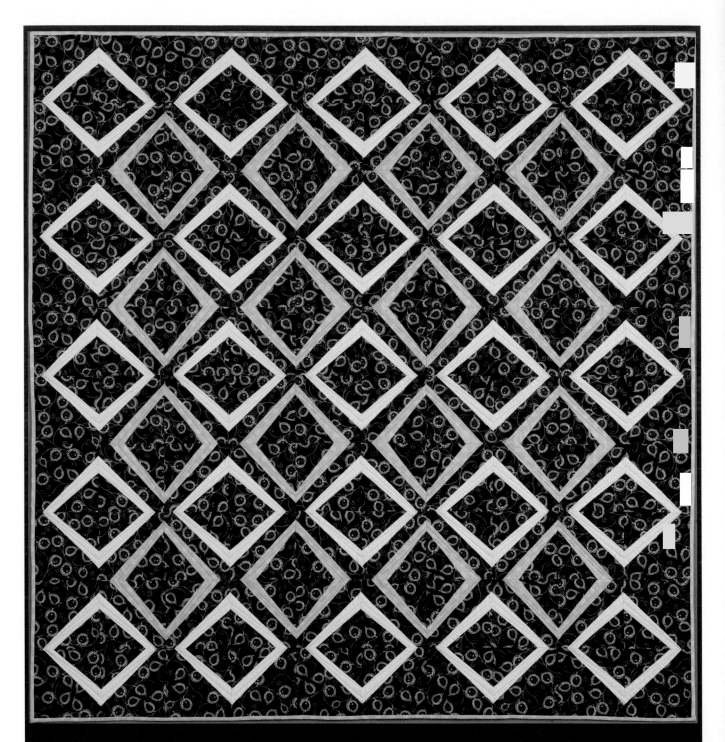

Designed by Denniele Bohannon
Pieced by Dianne Barnden, Paraparaumu, New Zealand
Quilted by Angela Walters

A Mother's Remembrance

Quilt Size: 60" x 60"
Paper-pieced
6" finished block

Fabric Requirements

- 1 ⅓ yards gray fabric
- 1 ⅓ yards yellow fabric (includes binding)
- 6 ¼ yards black fabric
- 4 yards backing

Additional Items

- 100 sheets of foundation paper
- Add-a-Quarter ruler (optional)

Almo's mother, Susie O'Kell.

It is clear that Almo was happy to roam all during his life. While he traveled far and wide, his mother, Susie, stayed firmly grounded in Quincy, Illinois, waiting for him to come home. Family stories paint a picture of her as a strong, loving mother who was forced to cope with great loss.

Red poppies and blue forget-me-nots remind us of the sacrifices made by the men and women who have served our country.

Since 1922, members of the VFW have sold red poppies on Veteran's Day. The proceeds provide support for veteran services and welfare. The Disabled American Veterans of the World War, officially organized on September 25, 1921, had their first Forget-Me-Not Day in 1926. Argonne Day on Sept. 26 and Armistice Day on Nov. 11 are the official blue forget-me-not dates.

A blue forget-me-not, sold by the DAVWW, was found tucked into Townsend O'Kell's (Almo's son) baby book.

A MOTHER'S REMEMBRANCE

CUTTING DIRECTIONS

From the gray fabric, cut:

- 100 – 1 ¾" x 9" rectangles (B)

From the yellow fabric, cut:

- 64 – 1 ¾" x 9" rectangles (C)

From the black fabric, cut:

- 36 – 7" squares (A)
- 128 – 5 ¼" x 6 ½" rectangles - With right sides together, cut once diagonally from corner to corner (D and Dr).
- 64 – 2 ¼" x 10 ½" rectangles (E)

CONSTRUCTION

Blocks 1 and 2

- Make 18 copies of each pattern on foundation paper. You will find the patterns on pages 84 and 85. Be sure to save the piece you trim off of the black A square. It is used as piece F.

Blocks 3 and 4

- Make 32 copies of each pattern on foundation paper. You will find the patterns on pages 86 and 87.

Paper-piece the blocks. The numbers indicate the sequence; the letters indicate the piece used.

Trim the blocks to 6 ½". Using the numbered grid as a guide, stitch ten blocks together to form a row. Refer to the diagram, and sew the rows together to complete the quilt top.

Note: Some of the blocks will need to be turned in their final placement. The numbered grid on page 67 shows the exact placement.

1	2	1	2	1	2	1	2	1	2
2	3	4	3	4	3	4	3	4	1
1	4	3	4	3	4	3	4	3	2
2	3	4	3	4	3	4	3	4	1
1	4	3	4	3	4	3	4	3	2
2	3	4	3	4	3	4	3	4	1
1	4	3	4	3	4	3	4	3	2
2	3	4	3	4	3	4	3	4	1
1	4	3	4	3	4	3	4	3	2
2	1	2	1	2	1	2	1	2	1

Designed and Pieced by Denniele Bohannon
Quilted by Angela Walters

Gold Star Patriot

Quilt size: 70" x 70"
Block Size: 12" Finished

Fabric Requirements

- 4 ¼ yards white
- 13" x 20" each of 25 assorted blues
- ⅔ yard blue (binding)
- 1 yard gold
- 4 ⅔ yards (backing)

During World War I, it became customary to hang service banners in the windows of homes that had someone actively serving. The banner was designed and patented by U.S. Army Captain Robert L. Queisser of the 5th Ohio Infantry in 1917 to honor his two sons fighting on the front lines.

The banner boasted a blue star on a white field surrounded by red. The star(s) indicated that someone living in the home was actively serving in the military. If that person was killed or died while serving, a smaller gold star was appliquéd over the blue.

GOLD STAR PATRIOT

CUTTING DIRECTIONS

From the white fabric, cut:
- 100 – 3 ½" squares (A)
- 100 – 3 ½" x 6 ½" rectangles (B)
- 40 – 12 ½" x 2" (sashing rectangle)
- 7 – 2 ½" strips x WOF (border)

From each of the 25 assorted blue fabrics, cut:
- 8 – 3 ½" squares (C)
- 4 – 2" x 3 ½" rectangles (E)
- 4 – 2" squares (D)

From the gold fabric, cut:
- 25 – 3 ½" squares (A)
- 216 – 2" squares (F and cornerstones)

CONSTRUCTION

To make each block, draw a diagonal line on the wrong side of eight gold F squares. With right sides together, place a gold F square on a blue E rectangle. Stitch on the drawn line. Trim off the corner leaving a ¼" seam. Press and repeat on the opposite end, creating a flying-geese unit. Make four.

Stitch a flying geese unit to opposite sides of a gold A square.

Stitch a blue D square to both ends of a flying geese unit. Make two. Sew these units to the remaining sides creating the center star.

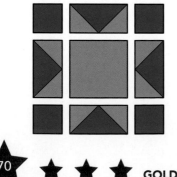

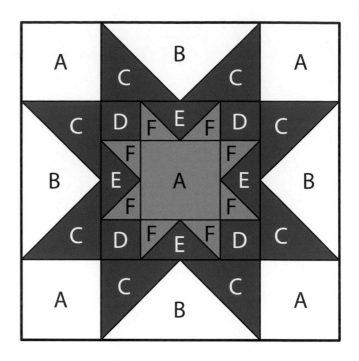

Draw a diagonal line on the wrong side of eight blue C squares. With right sides together, place a blue C square on a white B rectangle. Stitch on the drawn line. Trim off the corner leaving a ¼" seam. Press and repeat on the opposite end creating a flying geese unit. Make four.

Stitch a flying geese unit to opposite sides of the pieced star square.

Stitch a white A square to both ends of a flying geese unit. Make two. Sew these units to the remaining sides creating the double star. Make 25 blocks.

Refer to the diagram below, and sew five blocks and four sashing strips together to make a row. Make five. Refer to the diagram, and sew five white sashing rectangles and four gold cornerstones together, alternating the pieces to make a row. Make four. Alternate a star row with a sashing row to assemble the top.

Stitch the 2 ½"-wide border strips together. Measure the length of the quilt. Cut two border pieces this length, and stitch one to either side of the center. Measure the width of the quilt, and cut the remaining two border pieces. Sew one to the top and the other to the bottom of the quilt.

Layer the quilt with batting and backing. Quilt and bind.

Stars and Stripes Table Runner

Quilt size: 10" x 54"

Designed by Denniele Bohannon

Pieced and Quilted by Denniele Bohannon and Janice Britz

Fabric Requirements

- 20" x 24" cream fabric
- 24" x 18" red fabric
- 12" square blue fabric
- ⅔ yard backing fabric
- 11" x 55" piece of batting

A scrap of newsprint Almo had saved from an old Stars and Stripes newspaper inspired our table runner. He sent an article that praised Field Hospital No. 3 home to his mother with a message scrawled across the top that said, "This from the paper - My Company. Mama, trim this and have it put in the Quincy paper saying [if] they're good with this." — Almo

CUTTING INSTRUCTIONS

From the cream fabric, cut:

- 4 – 2 ½" x 22 ½" rectangles
- 7 stars using the star template

From the red fabric, cut:

- 6 – 2 ½" x 22 ½" rectangles

From the backing fabric, cut:

- 2 – 11" x 28" rectangles

CONSTRUCTION

Arrange the seven cream stars in a circle on the 12" blue square. Using your favorite appliqué method, stitch the stars in place and trim the square to 10 ½".

Stitch three red and two cream rectangles together alternating the colors. Make two.

Sew a strip set to either side of the center blue square.

Sew the two pieces of backing fabric together along the short end. Press the seams open.

Layer the batting and the backing together with right sides up. Place the top of the runner face down on the batting. Stitch around the outer edge, leaving approximately 4" open for turning.

Turn the runner right side out and press. Hand stitch the opening closed.

For the curved end version, follow the above instructions, but before you layer and stitch the front and back together, use the end template to mark the stitching lines on the wrong side of the top. Trim the excess fabric away from the marked line. Layer the backing, batting and top as described above, and stitch around the outer edge leaving about 4" open for turning purposes. Turn right side out, and stitch the opening closed.

Quilt as desired.

You will find the templates on page 89.

Poppy Pin

Designed and Pieced
by Denniele Bohannon

Fabric Requirements

- 4" x 12" piece of orange wool
- 1" scrap of green wool

Additional supplies

- #6 Perle cotton thread to match fabric
- Clasp

CUTTING DIRECTIONS

From the orange wool, cut:

- 1 top petal using the template provided
- 2 bottom petals using the template provided

From the green wool, cut:

- 1 center using the template provided

CONSTRUCTION

Refer to the diagram below, and layer the top petal with a bottom petal. Stitch as shown using a buttonhole stitch.

Place the green wool center in the middle of the flower. Stitch in place, and fill the center using a satin stitch. Add a French knot in the middle, and scatter French knots around the outer edge of the center.

Place on top of the second bottom petal, and sew around the entire outer edge with a buttonhole stitch. Sew the clasp to the back. You will find the templates on page 90.

Poppy Pincushion

Designed and Stitched by Denniele Bohannon
Finished Size: 6" square

Fabric Requirements

- 3 ½" x 7" piece orange wool
- 6 ½" square cream wool
- 6 ½" square green wool
- 7" x 14" piece of muslin
- 6 ½" square wool for backing

Additional supplies

- ½" green button
- 2 cups ground nuts shells or other filling material

CUTTING DIRECTIONS

From the orange wool, cut:
- 1 top petal using the template provided
- 1 bottom petal using the template provided

From the green wool, cut:
- 1 frame using the template provided

From the muslin, cut:
- 2 – 6 ½" squares

CONSTRUCTION

Refer to the photo, and layer the orange wool petals in place. Pin the petals to the cream square. Stitch around the petals using a buttonhole stitch.

Place the green wool frame on top of the cream square. Stitch around the inside of the frame using a buttonhole stitch.

Sew the green ½" button to the center of the poppy.

Place the cream square with the poppy right side up. Add the two 6 ½" muslin squares and the 6 ½" wool-backing square on top of the cream. Stitch around the outside using a ¼" seam allowance. Leave a 3" opening for turning and stuffing.

Turn the pincushion right side out. Carefully add the filling material between the two muslin layers. Stitch the inner muslin lining closed. Sew the outside wool cover closed to complete the pincushion. You will find the templates on pages 90 and 91.

Templates

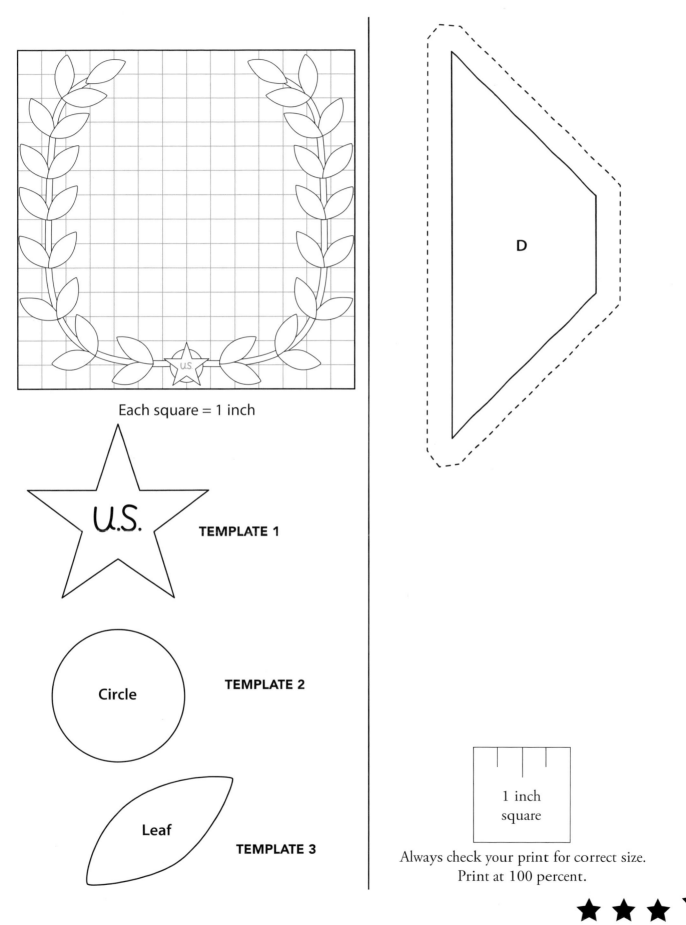

Each square = 1 inch

D

U.S. TEMPLATE 1

Circle TEMPLATE 2

Leaf TEMPLATE 3

1 inch
square

Always check your print for correct size.
Print at 100 percent.

77

BLOCK 3

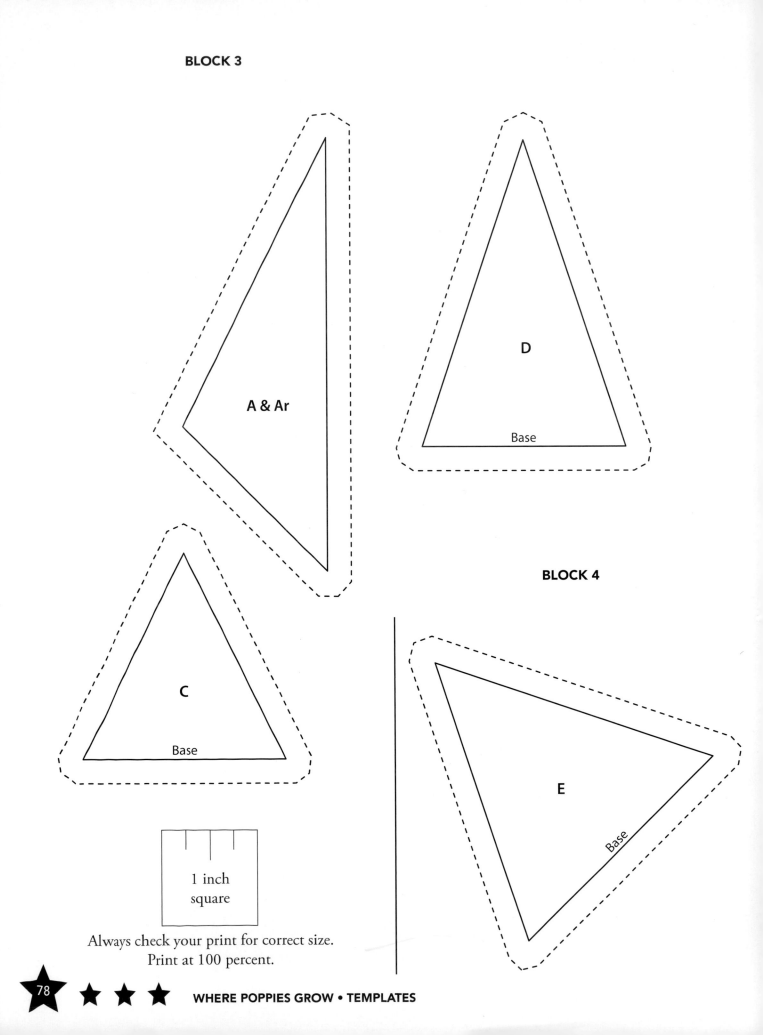

A & Ar

D

Base

BLOCK 4

C

Base

E

Base

1 inch square

Always check your print for correct size.
Print at 100 percent.